Date: 4/12/17

J 978.8 HAM
Hamilton, John,
Colorado : the Centennial State /

COLORADO

The Centennial State

BY
JOHN HAMILTON

Abdo & Daughters
An imprint of Abdo Publishing | abdopublishing.com

abdopublishing.com

Published by ABDO Publishing, a division of ABDO, PO Box 398166, Minneapolis, Minnesota 55439. Copyright © 2017 by Abdo Consulting Group, Inc. International copyrights reserved in all countries. No part of this book may be reproduced in any form without written permission from the publisher. ABDO & Daughters™ is a trademark and logo of ABDO Publishing.

Printed in the United States of America, North Mankato, Minnesota.
012016
092016

Editor: Sue Hamilton   **Contributing Editor:** Bridget O'Brien
Graphic Design: Sue Hamilton
Cover Art Direction: Candice Keimig   **Cover Photo Selection:** Neil Klinepier
Cover Photo: iStock
Interior Images: Airport-Technology, Alamy, AP, Colorado Avalanche, Colorado Dept of Transportation, Colorado Geological Survey, Colorado Rockies, Corbis, Denver Broncos, Denver International Airport, Denver Nuggets, Denver Zoo, ESPN, Frederic Remington, Getty, Granger Collection, History in Full Color-Restoration/Colorization, iStock, Jack Roberts/Glenwood Hot Springs Lodge, John Hamilton, Library of Congress, Mile High Maps, Minden Pictures, National Science Foundation, Northern Colorado Water Conservancy District, Red Rocks Park and Ampitheatre, Rick Kimpel, U.S. Dept of Agriculture, Wark Photography, Wikimedia.

Statistics: *State and City Populations*, U.S. Census Bureau, July 1, 2014 estimates; *Land and Water Area*, U.S. Census Bureau, 2010 Census, MAF/TIGER database; *State Temperature Extremes*, NOAA National Climatic Data Center; *Climatology and Average Annual Precipitation*, NOAA National Climatic Data Center, 1980-2015 statewide averages; *State Highest and Lowest Points*, NOAA National Geodetic Survey.

Websites: To learn more about the United States, visit booklinks.abdopublishing.com. These links are routinely monitored and updated to provide the most current information available.

Cataloging-in-Publication Data

Names: Hamilton, John, 1959- author.
Title: Colorado / by John Hamilton.
Description: Minneapolis, MN : Abdo Publishing, [2016] | The United States of America | Includes index.
Identifiers: LCCN 2015957506 | ISBN 9781680783087 (print) | ISBN 9781680774122 (ebook)
Subjects: LCSH: Colorado--Juvenile literature.
Classification: DDC 978.8--dc23
LC record available at http://lccn.loc.gov/2015957506

CONTENTS

THE CENTENNIAL STATE

P eople are always looking up in Colorado. The Rocky Mountains cover almost half the state. There are dozens of "14ers" (mountains higher than 14,000 feet (4,267 m)), more than any other state. The Colorado Plateau is filled with canyons and mesas. All across Colorado, there are minerals to be dug from the Earth, cattle to be rounded up, and trails to ride.

Colorado is growing fast. The state's big cities are booming with newcomers who arrive daily. They are attracted by growing businesses, pleasant weather, and adventures around every corner.

Colorado became a state in 1876, the same year the United States celebrated its 100th birthday. That is why it is known as "The Centennial State."

QUICK FACTS

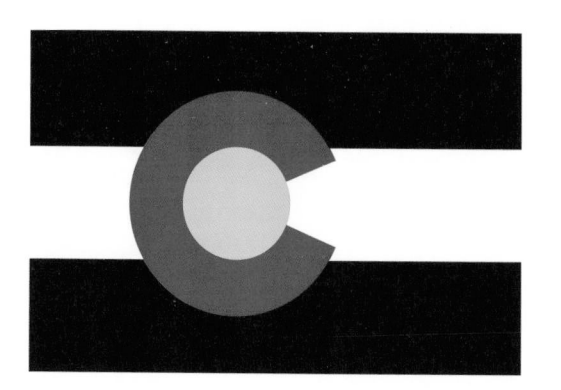

Name: Colorado is a Spanish word meaning "colored red." Early Spanish explorers named the Colorado River the Rio Colorado because of the reddish silt that gives the river its color.

State Capital: Denver, population 663,862

Date of Statehood: August 1, 1876 (38th state)

Population: 5,355,866 (22nd-most populous state)

Area (Total Land and Water): 104,094 square miles (269,602 sq km), 8th-largest state

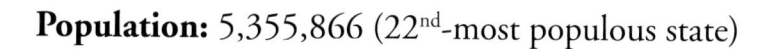

Largest City: Denver, population 663,862

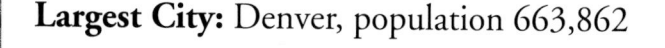

Nickname: The Centennial State

Motto: *Nil Sine Numine* (Nothing Without the Deity)

State Bird: Lark Bunting

Columbine

State Flower: White and Lavender Columbine

State Gemstone: Aquamarine

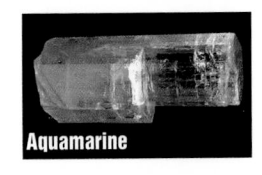
Aquamarine

State Tree: Colorado Blue Spruce

State Songs: "Where the Columbines Grow" and "Rocky Mountain High"

Blue Spruce

Highest Point: Mount Elbert, 14,440 feet (4,401 m)

Lowest Point: 3,315 feet (1,010 m) on the Arikaree River

Average July High Temperature: 83°F (28°C)

Mount Elbert

Record High Temperature: 114°F (46°C), in Las Animas on July 1, 1933, and Sedgwick on July 11, 1954

Average January Low Temperature: 13°F (-11°C)

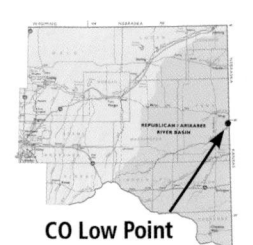
CO Low Point

Record Low Temperature: -61°F (-52°C), in Maybell on February 1, 1985

Average Annual Precipitation: 18 inches (46 cm)

Number of U.S. Senators: 2

Number of U.S. Representatives: 7

U.S. Postal Service Abbreviation: CO

GEOGRAPHY

Colorado is located in the American West. It shares borders with New Mexico and Oklahoma to the south. Nebraska wraps around Colorado's north and east side. Kansas is also to the east. Wyoming is also to the north, while Utah is to the west. Colorado is a "Four Corners" state. It shares its southwestern tip with Utah, Arizona, and New Mexico.

A marker shows where the four states meet up.

Colorado is the eighth-largest state. It covers 104,094 square miles (269,602 sq km). The state is rich with geographic features. They include arid plains, deserts, canyons, forests, and lakes. But Colorado is most famous for its mountains. The Rocky Mountains occupy almost half of the entire western side of the state.

Colorado has 58 peaks that soar over 14,000 feet (4,267 m). Mountain climbers like to reach the summits of these "14ers" for bragging rights. The most famous Colorado 14ers include Longs Peak, Mount Evans, and Pikes Peak.

Colorado has the highest average elevation of any state.

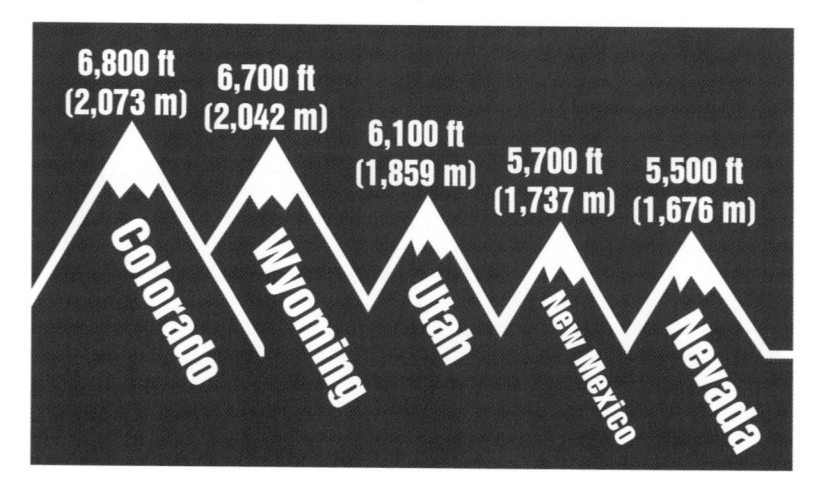

6,800 ft (2,073 m) — Colorado
6,700 ft (2,042 m) — Wyoming
6,100 ft (1,859 m) — Utah
5,700 ft (1,737 m) — New Mexico
5,500 ft (1,676 m) — Nevada

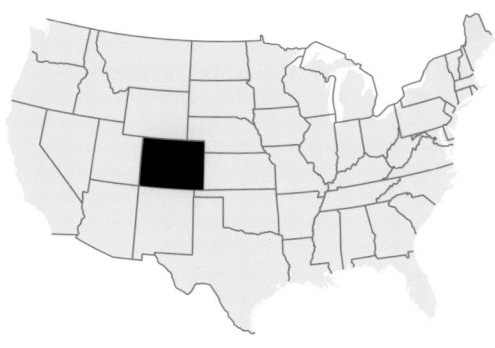

Colorado's total land and water area is 104,094 square miles (269,602 sq km). It is the 8th-largest state. The state capital is Denver.

GEOGRAPHY

Deep shadows inside the Black Canyon of the Gunnison make the steep cliffs of gneiss and schist appear black.

Colorado has many high plateaus. These large, flat places rise above the surrounding region. The Colorado Plateau is in the western and southwestern corner of the state. It contains rugged canyons and mesas. The bottom of the 2,722-feet (830-m) -deep Black Canyon of the Gunnison is so narrow that it receives only about 30 minutes of sunlight each day.

Colorado's eastern half contains flat, arid plains. Called the High Plains, they are part of the larger Great Plains of the United States. The region is well suited for cattle ranching and irrigation farming.

The Colorado Piedmont is a narrow strip of land that runs north and south. It is located between the mountains and the high plains. It is lower in elevation than the plains, and gets more water. Most of Colorado's major cities are located in the Piedmont. They include the Fort Collins, Denver, Colorado Springs, and Pueblo metropolitan areas.

Colorado has four major rivers. The Colorado River flows west into Utah. The Rio Grande flows south into New Mexico. The Arkansas River flows across southern Colorado into Kansas. The South Platte flows across northern Colorado. It runs through Denver on its way to Nebraska.

The South Platte River moves through Morgan County, Colorado, providing water for nearby farmland.

CLIMATE AND
WEATHER

Colorado's many different landforms greatly affect the state's weather. The plains of eastern Colorado are semi-arid. There is much sunshine and low humidity, but sometimes rain is so scarce it causes drought. Summer high temperatures are hot, while in winter the thermometer usually dips below freezing. Thunderstorms blow across the plains in summer, sometimes spawning tornadoes, large hail, or flash flooding. In winter, blizzards can be a hazard.

A spring rainstorm blows across the Colorado plains in El Paso County.

A cross-country skier sets out across snowy Colorado.

Compared to the plains, there is much more moisture in the Rocky Mountains. Altitude greatly affects temperature. There is greater precipitation on the westward slopes of the mountains. In winter, snow is so abundant that Colorado is home to many world-class ski resorts. In other mountainous places, precipitation is much less. The entire state averages only 18 inches (46 cm) of precipitation annually. When drought grips Colorado, wildfires are a danger.

In the Canyon and Plateau regions of western and southern Colorado, winters are not as harsh. Many areas are sunny and mild. Temperatures can reach 100°F (38°C) or more on summer afternoons in low-lying areas. Cooler temperatures are common at higher elevations.

PLANTS AND
ANIMALS

Shortgrass prairie covers much of Colorado's hot and dry eastern plains. Grama and buffalo grasses are common. There is also soapweed yucca, sagewort, and plains prickly pear cactus. In wet years, spring wildflowers bloom across the prairie. These include evening primrose, purple clover, blanketflower, wild indigo, spiderwort, sunflowers, and many more. Cottonwood and willow trees grow near the banks of lakes and rivers.

Yucca plants sprout on the prairie near Pawnee Buttes, Colorado.

Many small mammals and reptiles are found in eastern Colorado. They live in an environment with little water or shelter. Many make their homes underground. Common mammals include prairie dogs, black-tailed jackrabbits, American badgers, black-footed ferrets, striped skunks, desert cottontail rabbits, ground squirrels, gophers, and many types of mice. The largest mammals are pronghorn, white-tailed deer, coyotes, and foxes.

Fox

Reptiles and amphibians of the shortgrass prairie include Western box turtles, Great Plains skinks, collared lizards, Woodhouse's toads, prairie rattlesnakes, bull snakes, and many others.

Lark buntings and meadowlarks are common prairie birds. Other birds inhabiting Colorado's eastern skies include red-tailed hawks, prairie falcons, American kestrels, burrowing owls, greater prairie chickens, turkey vultures, and many other species.

Collared Lizard

Wildflowers abound in the Colorado foothills.

In the mountain foothills, common trees include oak, juniper, and piñon pine. Farther west, evergreen forests cover much of the Rocky Mountains. Common trees include Douglas fir, blue spruce, and Engelmann spruce. Groves of aspen are also found in large numbers. Covering the forest floor are grasses, ferns, and wildflowers. Columbine is Colorado's state flower.

Animals in the mountain forests include mule deer, elk, red foxes, martens, black bears, weasels, porcupines, cottontail rabbits, snowshoe hares, Abert's squirrels, yellow-bellied marmots, coyotes, bobcats, beavers, and mountain lions. Colorado's official state animal is the Rocky Mountain bighorn sheep.

Common birds found in western Colorado include ravens, jays, wild turkeys, hawks, bluebirds, grouse, hummingbirds, and woodpeckers. Golden and bald eagles are often seen soaring in the skies above.

At about 11,500 feet (3,505 m) or higher, trees cannot grow in Colorado. Above this "tree line," mosses, lichens, and small plants can be found. They are tough enough to endure the cold, harsh environment of the alpine tundra.

The Colorado Plateau is in the western and southwestern parts of the state. It is an arid, semidesert region. Only hardy plants and trees grow here, such as sagebrush, prickly pear cactus, piñon pine, yucca, juniper, plus many types of lichen and desert grasses. Animals found here include mountain lions, coyotes, foxes, badgers, skunks, prairie dogs, pronghorn, and mule deer.

Big horn sheep graze in Rocky Mountain National Park.

HISTORY

Native Americans have lived in Colorado for thousands of years. At Barger Gulch, northwest of Denver, archaeologists have found tools and other artifacts that are at least 10,500 years old.

The Anasazi people are also called the Ancestral Puebloans. (Anasazi is a Navajo word that means "ancient ones," or "ancient enemies.") They first came to the southwest corner of Colorado about 100 AD. They lived in pit houses partially dug out of the ground, or in square-roomed stone houses bunched together as pueblos, or towns. But the Anasazi are most famous for their multi-level homes built into the sides of cliffs.

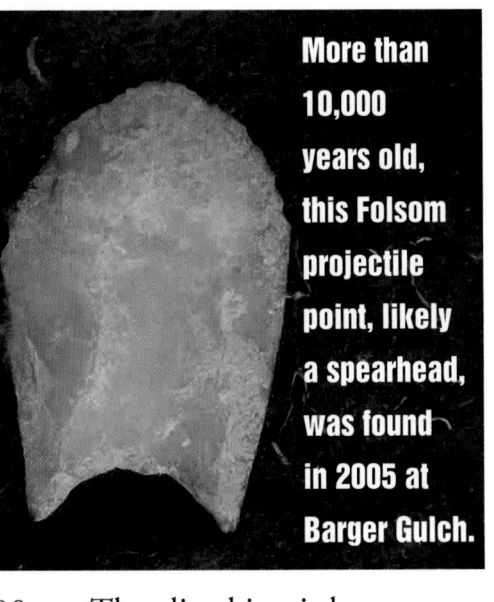

More than 10,000 years old, this Folsom projectile point, likely a spearhead, was found in 2005 at Barger Gulch.

Overhanging cliff walls gave protection from the elements. In war, the Anasazi could easily lift up ladders to prevent enemies from attacking. Many cliff dwellings can be seen today in southwestern Colorado. Protected sites include Canyons of the Ancients National Monument and Mesa Verde National Park.

Starting in the late 1200s, the Anasazi migrated away from their homes. They may have left because of warfare, or because of a severe drought. Many Pueblo people today, including the Hopi, trace their ancestors back to the Anasazi.

Mesa Verde, Spanish for "green table," is a protected site in southwest Colorado. The Ancestral Puebloans made the cliff dwellings their home from 600 to 1300 AD. Mesa Verde National Park protects nearly 5,000 known archeological sites, including 600 Anasazi cliff dwellings.

19

A Ute camp at Glenwood Hot Springs, by western artist Jack Roberts.

In the early 1500s, Spanish conquistadors were the first Europeans to explore Colorado. They came looking for gold. Spain soon claimed the Colorado area. It also claimed Mexico and most of the American Southwest region.

Despite Spain's claim of ownership, thousands of Native Americans already lived in Colorado. On the eastern plains were the Arapaho, Comanche, Kiowa, and Cheyenne tribes. The powerful Ute people lived in the Rocky Mountains. The Shoshone occupied parts of northern Colorado.

Colorado was so remote and mountainous that much of it remained unexplored by Europeans. In the 1600s and 1700s, Spain and France competed over who owned the land. By 1800, France claimed most of eastern Colorado. In 1803, France sold this land to the United States. It was part of a much larger area called the Louisiana Purchase.

Mountain men and fur traders such as James Pursley ventured into the Rocky Mountains of Colorado in 1804 and 1805. U.S. Army Captain Zebulon Pike led an organized expedition into Colorado in 1806 and 1807. The Pike Expedition explored much of Colorado's eastern plains and southern Rocky Mountains. Pikes Peak is named after Zebulon Pike. He and some of his men tried and failed to climb the 14,115-foot (4,302-m) mountain.

The Zebulon Montgomery Pike monument is in Pueblo, Colorado.

Military officer and explorer John Fremont hired mountain man Kit Carson to help guide his first expedition to the American West in the summer of 1842. The group explored many of Colorado's mountain passes.

Mexico won independence from Spain in 1821. It claimed all of Spain's former New World territories, including southern and western Colorado.

In the 1830s and 1840s, more American fur trappers and settlers came to eastern Colorado. They built Bent's Fort and Fort Pueblo on the Arkansas River. Fort Saint Vrain was built along the South Platte River. The forts provided shelter and supplies to fur traders. In the 1840s, John Fremont and Kit Carson explored many of Colorado's mountain passes.

In 1848, the two-year Mexican-American War came to an end. A peace treaty gave the victorious Americans much land, including the remaining parts of today's Colorado.

Miners seek their fortune during the Pikes Peak Gold Rush.

Ten years later, excitement in Colorado exploded with the discovery of gold. In 1858 and 1859, thousands of treasure seekers flooded into the state. Many mining towns sprang up, including Gold Hill, Black Hawk, and Central City. The gold rush was called the Pikes Peak Gold Rush because of the phrase "Pikes Peak or Bust!" Most of the gold camps, however, were well north of Pikes Peak.

Colorado proved very rich in gold and other minerals, such as silver. Cattle ranching and farming also grew. Colorado became the 38th state on August 1, 1876.

Mining is still important in Colorado, but the focus is no longer on gold. Oil, coal, and natural gas are prized resources today. Cattle ranching and tourism are also important.

DID YOU KNOW?

- Denver's nickname is "The Mile High City." Its elevation is 5,280 feet (1,609 m) above sea level, exactly one mile (1.6 km). A brass plaque on the capitol building's 13th step marks the mile-high spot. The mile-high point is also carved into the capitol's step.

- Great Sand Dunes National Park is located in south-central Colorado. It has the tallest sand dunes in all of North America. They were formed thousands of years ago by swirling winds from mountain passes. Sand from an ancient dried lakebed collected around the western base of the Sangre de Cristo Mountains. The tallest dune rises 755 feet (230 m) above the San Luis Valley. The largest dune field covers about 30 square miles (78 sq km).

- The largest silver nugget ever found in North America weighed more than one ton (.9 metric ton). It was pulled in 3 pieces from the Smuggler Mine near Aspen, Colorado, in 1894. It originally weighed 2,340 pounds (1,061 kg), and was made of 93 percent pure silver.

- The United States military has a base that is built *inside* one of Colorado's mountains. The Cheyenne Mountain Complex is part of the North American Aerospace Defense Command (NORAD). It is located near Colorado Springs. The base has equipment that can track enemy missiles. It was built underneath 2,000 feet (610 m) of granite mountain in the 1960s. Heavy shielding and 25-ton (23-metric-ton) blast doors protect against nuclear attack.

- Denver International Airport has the longest commercial aircraft runway in North America. It is Runway 16R/34L, which is 16,000 feet (4,877 m) long—approximately 3 miles (5 km).

PEOPLE

Margaret Brown (1867-1932) was born in Missouri, but moved to Leadville, Colorado, when she was a teenager. She married J.J. Brown in 1886. She and her husband became rich when the company he worked for, Ibex Mining Company, struck gold. Margaret Brown used her wealth to fight for women's rights. She gave to many charities that helped children and others in need. She was also active in the American Red Cross.

In early 1912, Brown was visiting France when she learned that her grandson had become ill. She took the first ship leaving for America—the RMS *Titanic*. When the ship struck an iceberg and sank, Brown helped evacuate fellow passengers. She earned the nickname, "Unsinkable Molly Brown."

Singer and songwriter **John Denver** (1943-1997) was one of the most popular musicians of the 1970s. He sold millions of albums worldwide. The son of a U.S. Air Force officer, he was born in New Mexico. His parents named him Henry John Deutschendorf, Jr. He learned to play guitar at age 11.

After finding early success in the mid-1960s, he changed his name to the capital city of the state he loved most, Colorado. He was inspired by the Rocky Mountains. Many of his songs were about nature and protecting the environment. He bought a house in Aspen, Colorado, and lived there much of his life. Denver was killed in a tragic plane crash in 1997. In 2007, one of his most famous songs, "Rocky Mountain High," became one of Colorado's two official state songs.

Melissa "Missy" Franklin (1995-) is a world-champion swimmer. She won four gold medals at the 2012 Summer Olympic Games in London, England. She also won a bronze medal. She has held speed records in the 100-meter and 200-meter backstroke and 4x100-meter medley relay. She has also won several world championships.

Franklin was born in Pasadena, California, but grew up in Centennial, Colorado, near Denver. She started swimming at age 5. "My mom was afraid of the water," Franklin said, "so she wanted me to learn early." Franklin is six foot one inch (185 cm) tall. Her nickname is "Missy the Missile." She trains at least two to four hours every day.

Chief Ouray (1833?-1880) was a leader of the Uncompahgre Ute tribe of Native Americans. He was a skilled diplomat. He tried to find peaceful ways for Native Americans and European settlers to live together. He was born in New Mexico, but came to Colorado at age 17. His name means "the arrow." He became chief at age 27.

Chief Ouray could speak Ute, English, Spanish, and Apache. This helped him negotiate peace treaties. Sadly, the discovery of gold and silver in Colorado meant the Ute people were forced out of their Rocky Mountain lands onto reservations in Utah. Chief Ouray died in 1880 while trying to negotiate peace for his people. The city of Ouray, Colorado, is named in his honor.

PEOPLE

CITIES

Denver is Colorado's capital. It is also the state's largest city. It has a
population of 663,862. Together with its suburbs, the Denver metro
area is home to more than three million people. Denver's elevation is
5,280 feet (1,609 m) above sea level, which is exactly one mile (1.6 km).
That is why its nickname is "The Mile High City." Denver started as a
mining town in 1858. Today, the city hosts many advanced-technology
companies in industries such as telecommunications, aerospace, and
computer software. The University of Colorado Denver is the state's
largest research university. Denver is also home to several professional
sports teams, world-class museums, a botanic garden, and a zoo.

Downtown Colorado Springs

Garden of the Gods

U.S. Air Force Academy

Colorado Springs is about 50 miles (80 km) south of Denver. It has a population of 445,830. The city is a center of high-tech industry and tourism. There are many natural wonders nearby. These include towering Pikes Peak and the red sandstone pillars of Garden of the Gods. Nearby is Peterson Air Force Base, the U.S. Army's Fort Carson, and the U.S. Air Force Academy. The city is home to the University of Colorado Colorado Springs. It also hosts a U.S. Olympic Training Center.

Pueblo is in south-central Colorado. The Arkansas River runs through the city. Its population is 108,423. It started as a trading post called Fort Pueblo in the 1840s. Today, Pueblo is an important center for manufacturing and trucking services for nearby farms and ranches. It is also a large producer of steel.

Fort Collins is north of Denver, near the Wyoming border. Its population is 156,480. The city began as a U.S. Army fort in 1864. Today, the city is a center for high-tech industries, agriculture, and tourism. Colorado State University enrolls more than 30,000 students.

Boulder's population is 105,112. It is nestled against
a mountain formation called the Flatirons. The city's name comes
from the boulders in Boulder Creek. The University of Colorado Boulder is
one of the largest universities in the state. It enrolls about 30,000 students.

Boulder is famous for its young population and for outdoor recreation.
The city also has a thriving arts community. The famous Pearl Street Mall
is a pedestrian-only shopping destination filled with restaurants, shops,
and street performers.

CITIES

TRANSPORTATION

Three main interstate highways crisscross Colorado. Interstate 25 goes north and south. It roughly follows the foothills of the Rocky Mountains. The mountains are to its west, and the plains are to its east. It passes through the major cities of Fort Collins, Denver, Colorado Springs, and Pueblo.

Interstate 70 follows an east-west path. Starting from the Kansas border, it travels west until it passes through Denver. From there, I-70 travels across the Rocky Mountains and through the Colorado Plateau until crossing into Utah.

Interstate 76 enters northeast Colorado from Nebraska. It travels southwest across the plains until ending in Denver.

About 60 miles (97 km) west of Denver on I-70, the interstate travels right through a mountain. The westbound Eisenhower Memorial Tunnel was finished in 1973. The eastbound Edwin C. Johnson Memorial Tunnel was completed in 1979. They are about 2 miles (3 km) long.

Denver International Airport

Denver International Airport's unusual "peaked" roof is designed to show both a feeling of snow-capped mountains, as well as Native American teepees on the Great Plains.

Denver International Airport is one of the busiest airports in the United States and the world. It was completed in 1995. More than 53 million passengers travel through the airport each year. It occupies more area than any other airport in the country. It covers about 53 square miles (137 sq km) of land on the eastern outskirts of Denver.

TRANSPORTATION

NATURAL
RESOURCES

Colorado's eastern plains are used heavily for farms and cattle grazing. This part of the state gets little rainfall. Much of the land is irrigated by pipes or ditches. Most of the water originally fell on the western side of the Rocky Mountains. The Alva B. Adams Tunnel diverts water from the Colorado River to the eastern plains. The tunnel runs more than 13 miles (21 km) under Rocky Mountain National Park. About 86 percent of irrigated water in Colorado is used for agriculture.

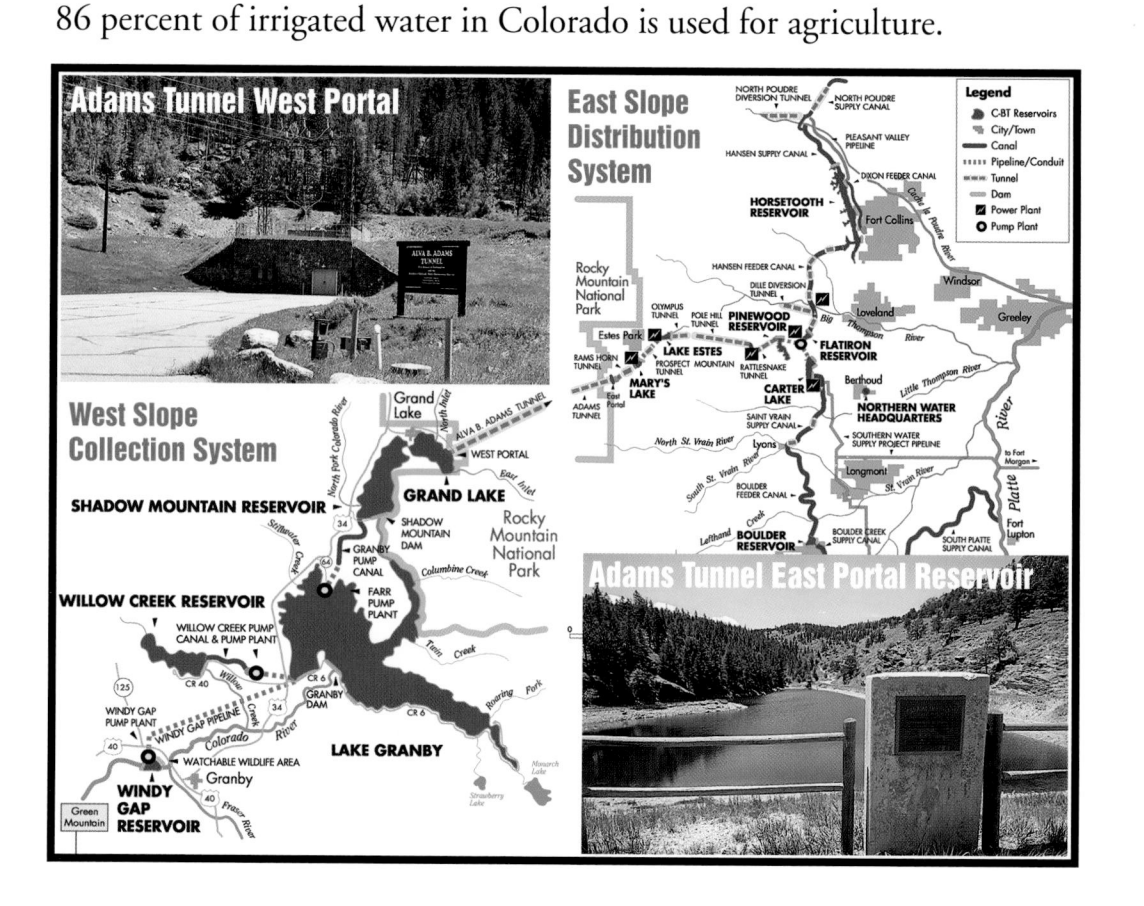

Oil Pump Jack

People once flocked to Colorado to mine gold and silver. Today, fossil fuels are more important. The state has big deposits of oil, natural gas, and coal. Many of these energy resources are found on the eastern plains. Seven of the country's 100 largest natural gas fields are in Colorado.

Colorado is the seventh-biggest producer of coal in the United States. The state mines 36.1 million tons (32.7 million metric tons) each year. Most is used to generate electricity. Oil shale is found in the northwest corner of Colorado. New technology in recent years helps extract oil and gas from these huge deposits. Other Colorado resources include uranium, molybdenum, gold, plus sand and gravel.

Coal Plant

NATURAL RESOURCES

INDUSTRY

The agriculture industry is very important to Colorado. Corn, wheat, and hay are grown on the eastern plains. Fruits and vegetables are harvested in the western part of the state. Cattle ranching accounts for almost half of all farm income. Colorado has 11,600 farms that raise cattle. Each year, the state has about 2.65 million head of cattle, which are worth more than $2.8 billion.

Colorado factories produce equipment used to make computers, robotics, and telecommunications devices. Other goods include transportation equipment, machinery, wood and paper products, plus military and aerospace equipment.

Tourists have their photo taken on the Pikes Peak Cog Railway. A cog, or rack, railroad is designed to climb steep inclines. Colorado's Pikes Peak Cog Railway is the highest rack railway in the world. It takes visitors near the summit of Pikes Peak, which has an altitude of 14,115 feet (4,302 m).

Tourism is a huge part of Colorado's economy. People flock to the state's world-class ski resorts, national and state parks, and bustling cities. More than 30 million visitors come to Colorado each year. They spend more than $10 billion at restaurants, hotels, parks, and other attractions. The tourism industry employs almost 150,000 people in Colorado.

The federal government is another big Colorado employer. There are several big military bases and federal government facilities in the state. Also, many big private employers, such as Lockheed Martin Space Systems, work directly with the government.

SPORTS

Colorado is the least-populated state to have teams in all four major league sports. Each team plays in the large Denver metropolitan area. The Denver Broncos are in the National Football League. They have won three Super Bowls. The Colorado Rockies represent Major League Baseball. The Denver Nuggets play in the National Basketball Association. The Colorado Avalanche play in the National Hockey League. The franchise has won two Stanley Cup Finals.

Other professional sports in the state include soccer, lacrosse, golf, rodeo, and automobile racing. College sports are also big in Colorado. The Colorado Buffaloes play a variety of sports at the University of Colorado Boulder. The Colorado State Rams are in Fort Collins. The University of Denver Pioneers are in Denver, and the United States Air Force Academy Falcons play in Colorado Springs.

Outdoor sports are hugely popular in Colorado. They include mountain climbing, hiking, biking, golfing, canoeing, kayaking, hunting, and camping. In the winter, skiing is a major pastime. Snowmobiling and snowshoeing are also popular.

Some people need an adrenaline rush with their sports, and Colorado has much to offer. Adventure sports found in the state include kayaking, mountain biking, rodeo, mountain climbing, hang gliding, whitewater rafting, and BASE jumping.

SPORTS

ENTERTAINMENT

The Denver Zoo was founded in 1896. Today, it covers 80 acres (32 ha). It is home to more than 619 kinds of animals, including 23 endangered species. Nearly two million people visit the zoo each year to see gorillas, giraffes, lions, bears, elephants, and many other animals.

The Denver Museum of Nature & Science has more than one million objects in its collections. Exhibits about the natural world highlight dinosaurs, space, Egyptian mummies, wildlife, geology, and more.

Other Colorado museums include the Ghost Town Museum in Colorado Springs, the Colorado Springs Fine Arts Center, the Aspen Art Museum, the Denver Art Museum, and Denver's Kirkland Museum of Fine & Decorative Art.

Denver Zoo's Toyota Elephant Passage opened in 2012.

Red Rocks Park

The world-famous Red Rocks Park contains a natural outdoor amphitheater west of Denver. It hosts many musical acts and special events. It is now a national historic landmark.

Colorado is home to four national parks. They include Rocky Mountain, Great Sand Dunes, Mesa Verde, and Black Canyon of the Gunnison National Parks. There are also many national monuments and state parks to explore.

ENTERTAINMENT

TIMELINE

1300—A long drought, or perhaps fighting with other tribes, forces the Ancestral Puebloan people (also known as the Anasazi) to leave their homes in Mesa Verde.

1500s—Spanish conquistadors are the first Europeans to explore today's Colorado. They come looking for gold. Spain claims the Colorado region.

1800—France claims most of eastern Colorado.

1803—The United States buys land from France. The Louisiana Purchase includes much of Colorado.

1804-1825—Frontiersmen, scouts, and fur traders explore Colorado.

1833—Bent's Fort, an important trading post, is built.

1848—After the Mexican-American War, the victorious United States takes possession of the remaining parts of today's Colorado.

1858-1859—Gold is discovered in several places in Colorado.

1870—Railroads connect Denver and Cheyenne, Wyoming.

1876—Colorado becomes the 38th state.

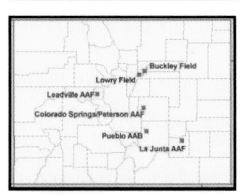

1941-1945—During World War II, the U.S. military builds several bases in Colorado.

1973—Eisenhower Tunnel is built beneath the Continental Divide 60 miles (97 km) west of Denver, making it easier to reach the ski slopes of western Colorado.

2001—The Colorado Avalanche win the National Hockey League Stanley Cup Finals.

2002-2019—ESPN's Winter X Games are held, or planned to be held, in Aspen, Colorado.

GLOSSARY

ADRENALINE

A chemical created in the human body that is released when a person feels strong emotions such as fear or excitement. Adrenaline causes the heart to beat faster and gives a person quick energy.

ANASAZI

Sometimes called the Ancestral Puebloans. They lived in the southwestern United States, including an area of Colorado, until about 1300 AD. They sometimes built their homes in the cliffs.

ARID

A very dry climate.

CONQUISTADORS

Spanish soldiers and explorers who came to the Americas in the 1500s. They used force to conquer native people and take control of their lands.

FOOTHILLS

Small hills where the land of the plains begins to rise into mountains.

GREAT PLAINS

The land east of the Rocky Mountains, west of the Mississippi River and stretching from Canada to the Mexican Border. It is mostly covered with grass and few trees.

Louisiana Purchase

A purchase by the United States from France in 1803 of a huge section of land west of the Mississippi River. The United States nearly doubled in size after the purchase. The young country paid about $15 million for more than 820,000 square miles (2.1 million sq km) of land.

Molybdenum

A silvery metal that melts only at a very high temperature. It is useful in making steel alloys used in armor, motors, electrical contacts, and aircraft parts.

New World

The areas of North, Central, and South America, as well as islands near these land masses. The term was often used by European explorers.

Piedmont

A long narrow strip of land in Colorado going north and south, between the mountains and the plains.

Plateau

A large, flat section of land that is raised up from the surrounding countryside. This area of high ground is mostly flat at the top.

Ute

A Native American tribe that lived in the mountains of Colorado before the Europeans came. Chief Ouray was an Uncompahgre Ute tribe leader.

World War II

A conflict that was fought from 1939 to 1945, involving countries around the world. The United States entered the war after Japan bombed the American naval base at Pearl Harbor, in Oahu, Hawaii, on December 7, 1941.

INDEX